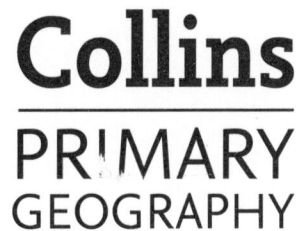

Investigation
Workbook 3

Planet Earth	**Landscapes**	
	The Earth's surface	2
	The shape of the land	4
	Investigating landscapes	6
Water	**Water around us**	
	A wet planet	8
	The effects of water	10
	Looking down at water	12
Weather	**Weather worldwide**	
	Different types of weather	14
	Living in hot and cold places	16
	Sunshine matters	18
Settlements	**Villages**	
	A village community	20
	Different types of village	22
	Investigating villages	24
Work and Travel	**Travel**	
	Ways of travelling	26
	Finding your way	28
	Routes and journeys	30
Environment	**Caring for nature**	
	Wildlife around us	32
	Protecting wildlife	34
	Working together	36
Places	**Scotland**	38
	France	44
	South America	50
	Asia	56

Daphne Paizee

Unit 1 Landscapes

Lesson 1: The Earth's surface

1 a) Look at the picture, which shows part of the Earth's surface. Label the picture using the words from the boxes.

rock   water   cloud   tree   mountain   animal

b) Why are air and water important on Earth?

_____

Unit 1 | **Landscapes**

❷ Look carefully at the satellite image of Earth taken from space. Answer the questions.

Hint: You can use a globe or an atlas.

a) Which continents can you see?

_____

b) What covers most of the surface of the Earth: land or water?

_____

c) Name the oceans and seas you can see in the photograph.

_____

d) What else does the photograph show?

_____

→ Supports Pupil Book Mapwork, page 3

Unit 1 Landscapes

Lesson 2: The shape of the land

1 Read the clues then find the words in the wordsearch puzzle.

a) a flat piece of land high up in the mountains _ _ _ _ _ _ _

b) like a mountain but not as high, with grass and trees _ _ _ _

c) low area in between hills, where rivers run _ _ _ _ _ _

d) area where the land meets the sea _ _ _ _ _

e) area of land surrounded by water _ _ _ _ _ _

f) flat land which is good for farming _ _ _ _ _

b	v	j	o	v	z	e
y	s	p	l	a	i	n
k	i	c	r	l	n	x
u	s	o	g	l	d	f
p	l	a	t	e	a	u
h	a	s	l	y	q	w
c	n	t	h	i	l	l
p	d	i	t	z	m	a

Unit 1 Landscapes

❷ Draw a map of an imaginary island with different landscapes. Label your map with the words from the boxes.

Hint: Look at the drawing on Pupil Book pages 4 and 5 to see these different landscapes.

coast   hills   mountains   valley   lowlands

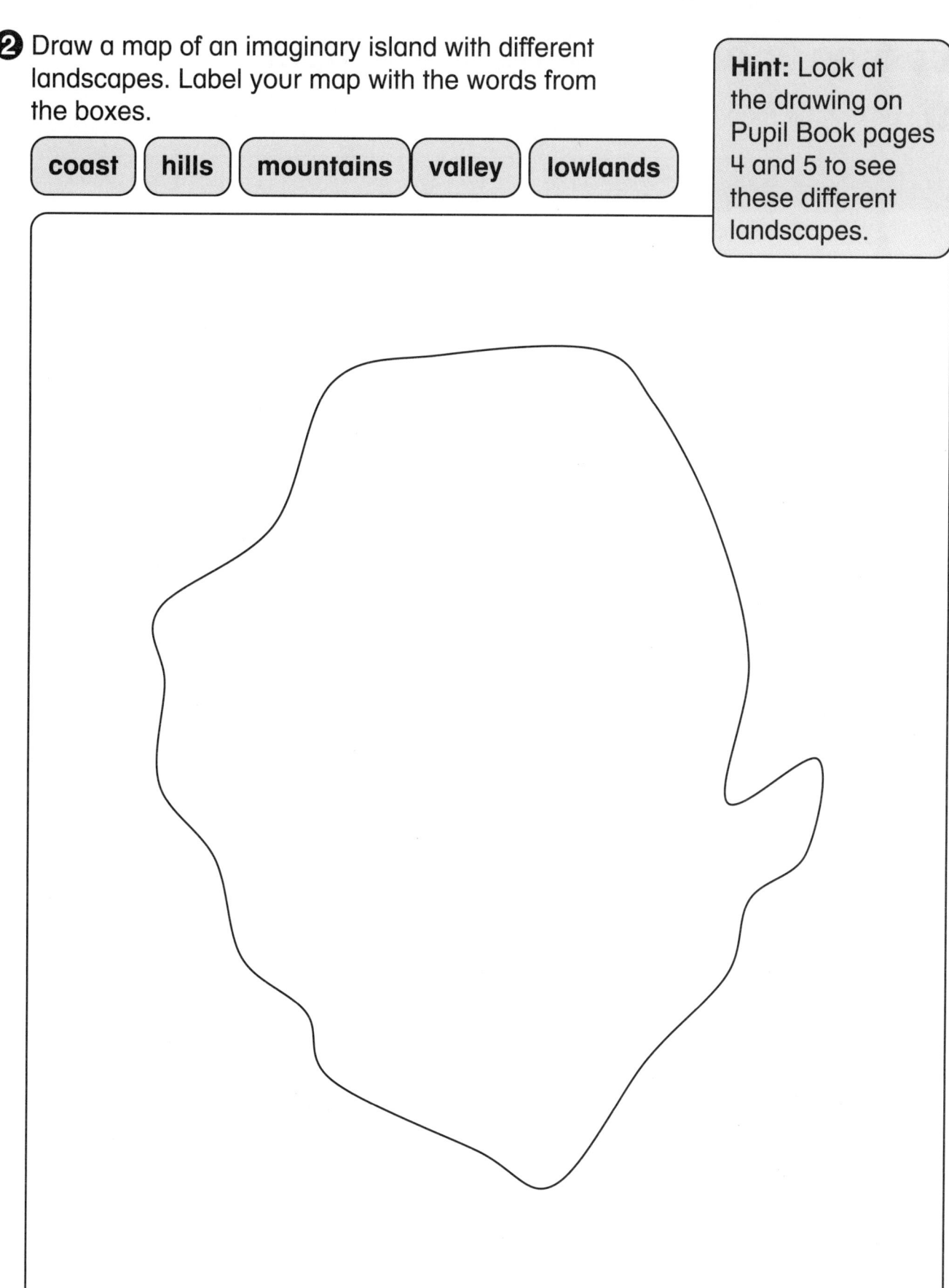

→ Supports Pupil Book Mapwork, page 4

Unit 1 — Landscapes

Lesson 3: Investigating landscapes

1 Look at the map of South America and answer the questions.

a) Make a list of the rivers on the map.

_____

b) Which mountain range is found down the western side of this continent?

_____

c) The Amazon River flows from the west to the east. Which ocean does it run into?

_____

d) Is South America mostly mountainous or mostly flat?

_____

Unit 1 **Landscapes**

2 a) Find photographs that show landscapes. For example: hill, mountain, river, lowland, sea, valley.

b) Stick the pictures in the boxes below and label them.

c) Write a caption to describe each landscape.

Hint: You can use the internet or magazines. Or you could draw pictures instead.

→ Supports Pupil Book Investigation, page 7

Unit 2 Water around us

Lesson 1: A wet planet

1 Each of the photographs below shows water on Earth.

   a) Name the water in each picture.

   b) Write a sentence to describe the water in each picture. Look at the example.

Waterfall

Liquid water in a river falls over steep rocks into the river below.

Unit 2   Water around us

❷ Draw a picture which shows water near where you live.

❸ Fill in this data about your picture.

Where is the water? (for example: the name of the place)	
What type of water is this? (for example: river, sea, snow, waterfall)	
Is the water liquid, solid or gas?	
Where does the water come from?	

Unit 2 Water around us

Lesson 2: The effects of water

1 Write a caption for each picture to say why water is important.

Fish live in water.

❷ How do people in your community use water? Complete the diagram by writing a different idea in each box.

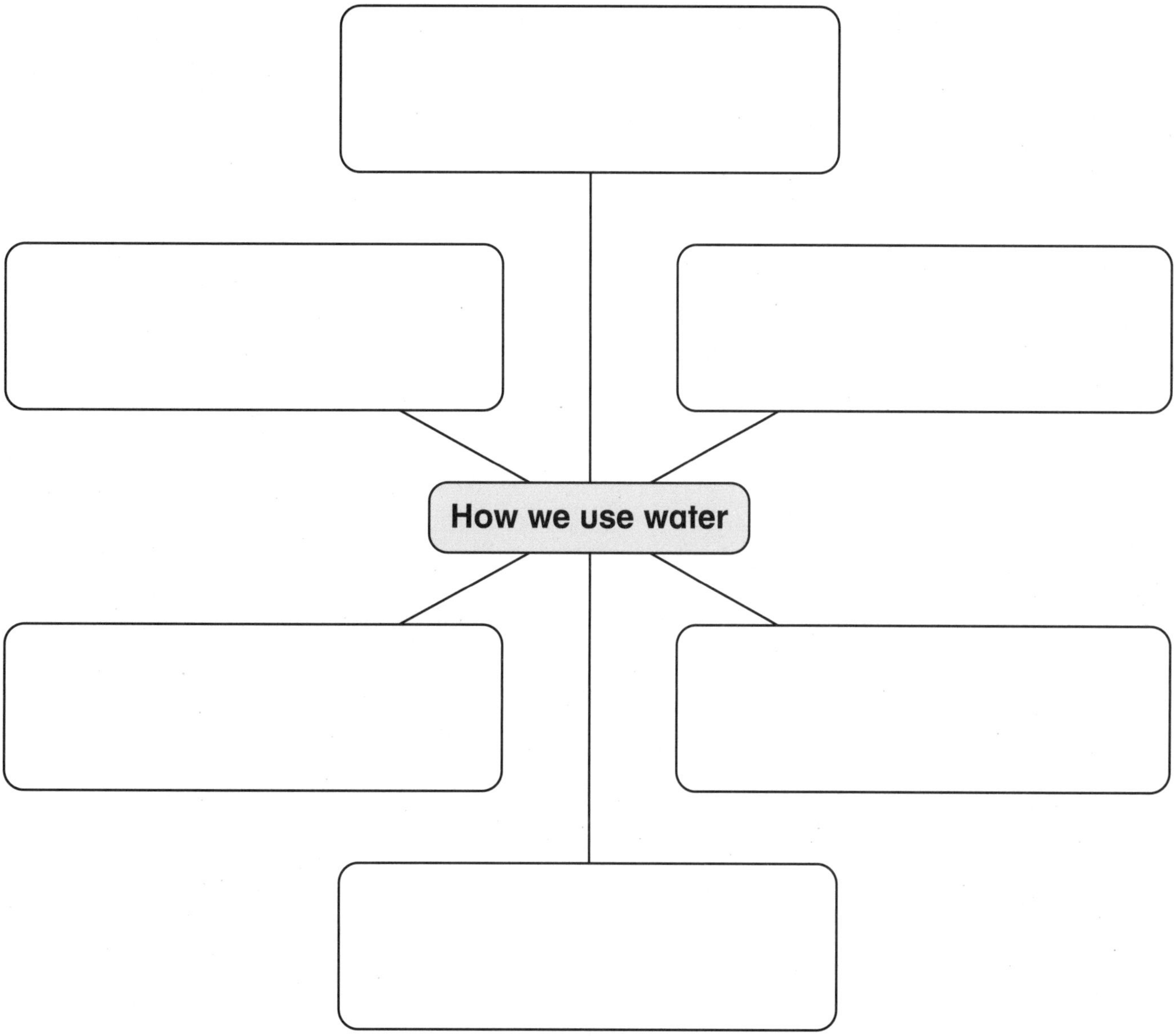

➜ Supports Pupil Book Mapwork, page 11

❸ How do you use water every day? Write three sentences.

____

____

____

❹ How can you save water? Write two ideas.

____

____

Unit 2 | Water around us

Lesson 3: Looking down at water

❶ Draw lines to match the words to their definitions.

- island
- marsh
- reservoir
- river
- satellite image

- a wet, muddy area
- flowing, fresh water
- a place where water is collected and kept
- a photograph taken from above
- an area of land with water around it

❷ Look at an atlas map of your country or continent. Make a list of the names of any rivers, lakes and seas or oceans you can find.

Rivers	Lakes	Seas and oceans

→ Supports Pupil Book Mapwork, page 12

Unit 2 | **Water around us**

❸ Complete the picture to show where rainwater goes in your school grounds. Your picture can include ideas from the words in the boxes.

| clouds | rain | down pipes | gutters |

| puddles | a stream | plants |

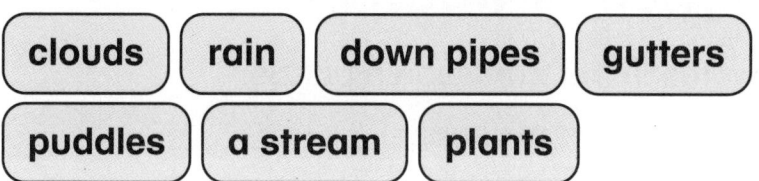

→ Supports Pupil Book Investigation, page 13

Unit 3　Weather worldwide

Lesson 1: Different types of weather

1 Read the clues then find the words in the wordsearch puzzle.

a) The pattern of weather over a number of years.　_ _ _ _ _ _ _

b) A place with a very dry, often very hot, climate.　_ _ _ _ _ _

c) A place that is hot and wet and where lots of trees, plants and animals are found.　_ _ _ _ _ _ _ _ _ _

d) The coldest places on Earth are _ _ _ _ _ lands.

e) Rain, sun and snow are different types of _ _ _ _ _ _ _.

f) Cold water turns to _ _ _ in cold places.

g) The temperature in the Amazon rainforest is always _ _ _.

o	i	c	e	r	q	e	m	d	h
c	u	l	x	w	p	k	g	e	o
r	a	i	n	f	o	r	e	s	t
z	l	m	y	g	l	p	t	e	x
s	v	a	n	b	a	m	i	r	h
k	d	t	r	j	r	f	z	t	w
v	w	e	a	t	h	e	r	u	a

2 Compare deserts and rainforests. Make notes in the table.

	Desert	Rainforest
What is the climate like?		
What does the landscape look like?		
Are there many plants and animals?		

Unit 3 Weather worldwide

3 a) Find or draw two colour pictures which show how climate change affects the weather.

For example:
- a heavy storm
- very dry land.

b) Write two sentences to describe each picture.

Think about these two questions:
- What do the colours in the picture tell us about the weather?
- How does the weather affect the plants and animals that live there?

_____

_____

_____

_____

→ Supports Pupil Book Climate change, page 15

Unit 3 Weather worldwide

Lesson 2: Living in hot and cold places

1 Look at the picture and think about what it is like to live in this place. Then answer the questions.

A community in a polar region.

a) What do you think the climate is like here?
   _____

b) Where do the people who live here get their food and water from?
   _____

c) How do people earn a living?
   _____

d) What clothing do people wear?
   _____

e) How do people move around?
   _____

f) Do you think the people keep animals like goats and cows? Give a reason.
   _____

Unit 3 Weather worldwide

❷ What problems could you face if you lived in a desert area or a polar land? What solutions are there to the problems?

Complete the table. Two examples have been done for you.

	Problems	Solutions
Desert area		collect and store water carefully
Polar land	very cold	

❸ What climate problems do you face where you live? What solutions do you have to deal with the problems?

_____

_____

_____

Unit 3 Weather worldwide

Lesson 3: Sunshine matters

❶ The diagram shows where the rays from the sun fall on Earth.
Use the words from the boxes to label the diagram.

sun's rays   air   Earth   North Pole
South Pole   sun   equator

❷ Which areas on Earth are the warmest? Use the diagram above to explain why they are the warmest areas.

_____
_____
_____

Unit 3 | **Weather worldwide**

3 a) Draw a picture of your school grounds.

b) Think about these questions:
- Which areas are hot?
- Which areas are cool?
- In which areas do plants grow well?
- Which areas provide shelter for creatures such as birds and insects?

c) Add a key to your picture. Use colours or patterns to show the different areas.

Key

hot	
cool	
good for plants	
shelter	

→ Supports Pupil Book Investigation, page 19

Unit 4 Villages

Lesson 1: A village community

1 Imagine that you live on another planet. How would you use the land on that planet? Fill in the land use map with pictures for different areas. Label each area.

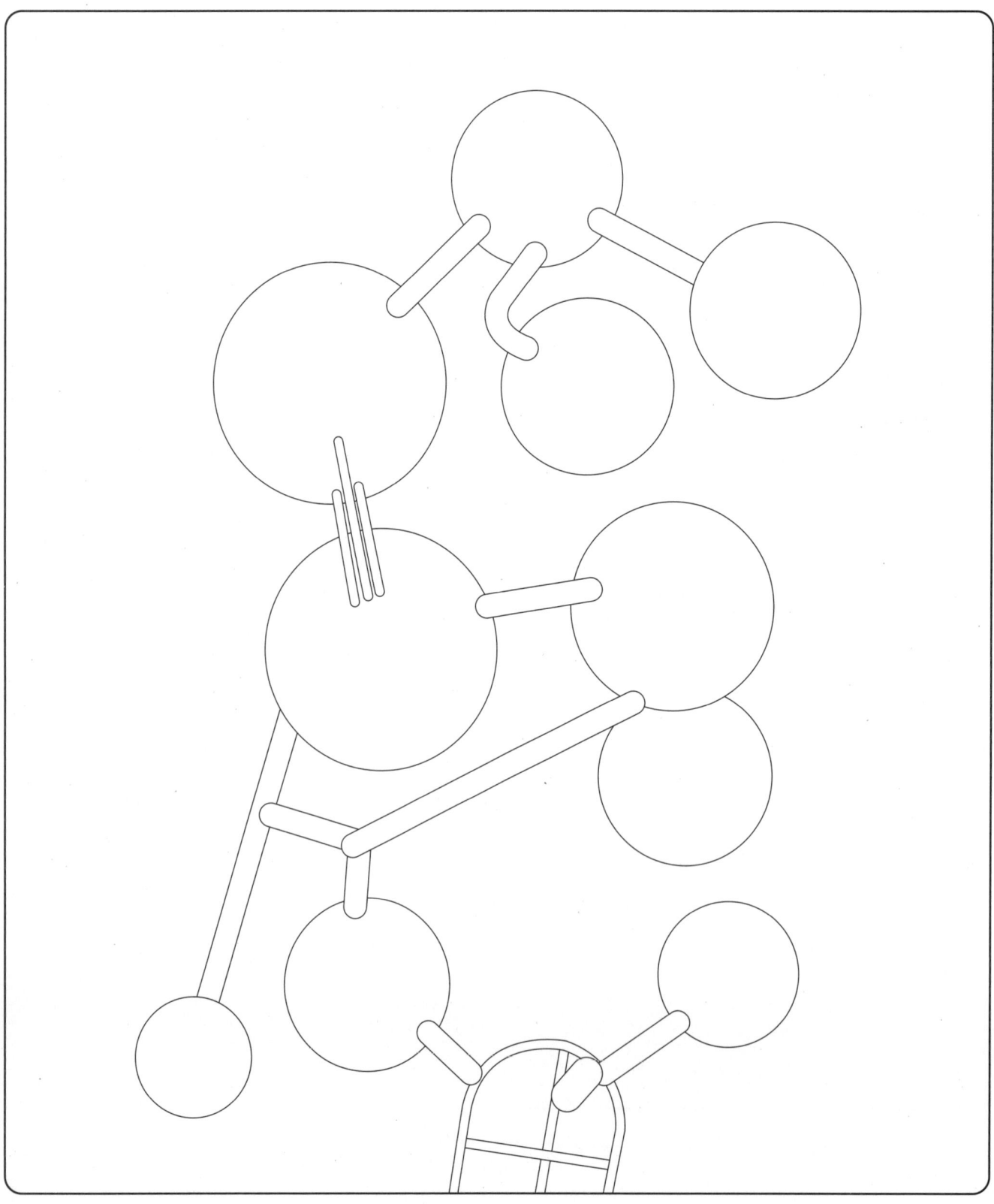

Unit 4   Villages

❷ Look at the images. How is the land used in each village?
Use the following words to label the land use in each picture.

| transport | farming | housing | meeting place |

| shopping | school |

Unit 4 Villages

Lesson 2: Different types of village

❶ Make a list of things people need when they look for the best place to live and build homes.

- _____
- _____
- _____
- _____
- _____

❷ Look at the photographs of the villages on page 23 of your Pupil Book.

Choose one photograph and draw a map of what you think the whole village looks like.

Think about these questions as you draw the map:
- Where do you think people could grow food?
- Where could people get water?
- How could people move around?
- Is there a place where they can relax, meet or play games?

Label places on the map.

Unit 4 Villages

❸ Research a village and complete a fact file.

a) Write three interesting facts or features about the village.

b) Stick in a photograph or draw a picture to add to your research. Give your picture a caption.

Fact file

Village's name: _____

Country: _____

Continent: _____

Fact 1: _____

Fact 2: _____

Fact 3: _____

What the picture shows: _____

Unit 4 Villages

Lesson 3: Investigating villages

1 What features would you find in a village near where you live? Draw small pictures of each feature. Label your pictures. Look at the example.

bus stop	_____	_____
_____	_____	_____
_____	_____	_____

Unit 4   Villages

❷ Do some research on a village.

> **Hint:** You may be able to find maps and information in a place such as a library or a tourist information centre. You can also talk to an older person who lives in a village, take photographs or make your own drawings.

a) Find or draw a picture of the village.

b) Draw a simple map of the village.

c) Add labels on your map.

→ Supports Pupil Book Investigation, page 25

Unit 5 Travel

Lesson 1: Ways of travelling

1 Draw lines to match the types of transport to the places they use.

bus and car	harbour
boat and ship	airport
aeroplane and helicopter	railway tracks
train	garage

2 Imagine that you live in a big city and you want to travel to another country. The country has lots of islands. You want to visit a forest on one of the islands. Which types of transport could you use to get there?

a) Draw pictures of the types of transport on the flow diagram below.

b) Write a sentence about each type of transport. Explain why you will use it.

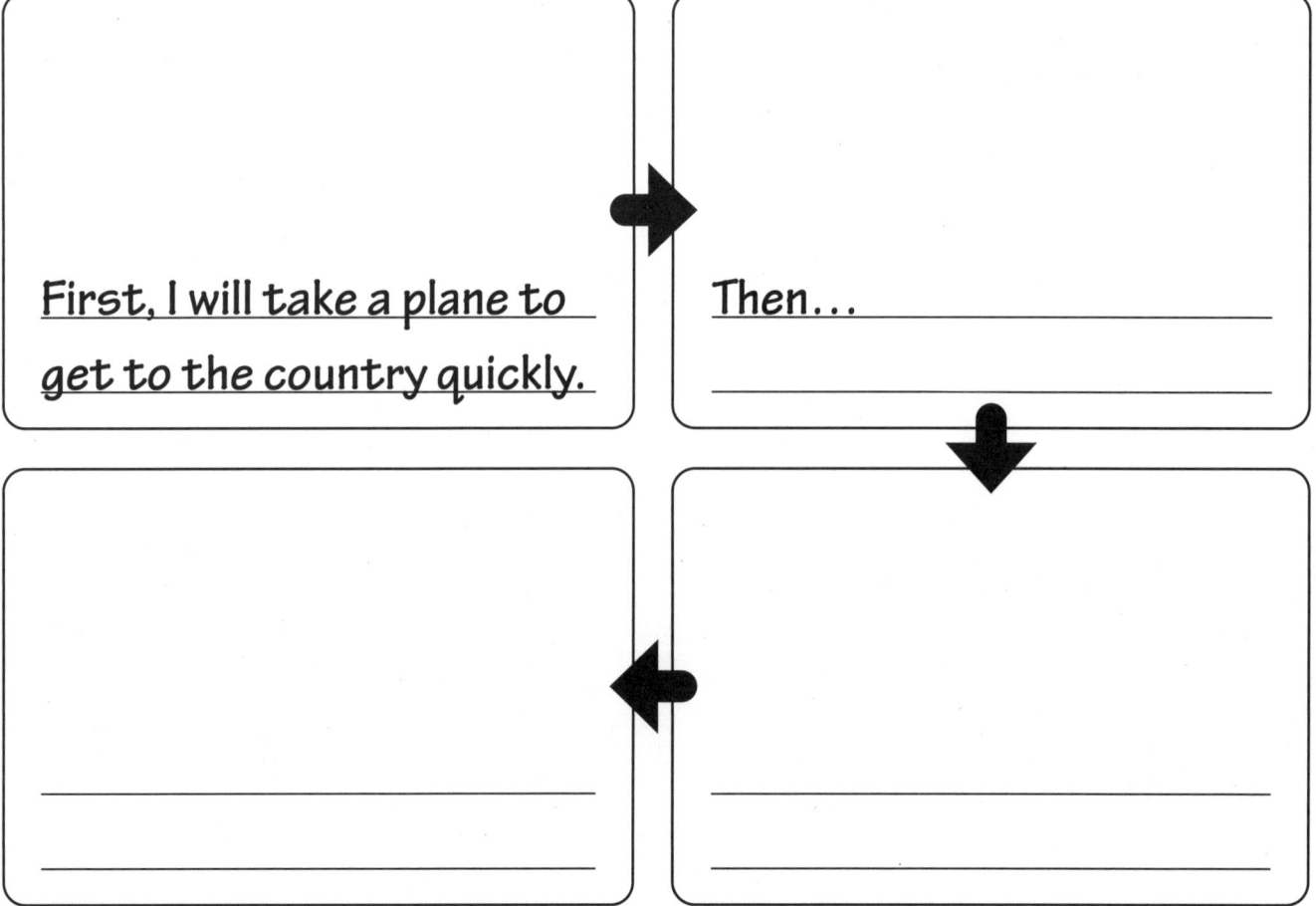

First, I will take a plane to get to the country quickly.

Then...

Unit 5 | Travel

3 Make a survey about how children in your class travel to school and travel around at weekends. Follow the steps to make the survey and record your results.

a) Step 1: Write the two questions you will ask.

b) Step 2: Write different types of transport as headings in the rows. Leave space to write more headings if needed.

c) Step 3: Ask each person both questions. Tick ✓ the correct column for each answer.

d) Step 4: Add up the ticks in each column.

Type of transport	Questions		Totals
	a) How do you travel to school?	b) _____	
Bus			
_____			
_____			
_____			
_____			

4 Write a few sentences about the results of your survey. Start like the example below. When you have finished, share your results.

I surveyed _____ children in my class. I asked them two questions about the type of transport they used. Most of the children travelled to school by _____.

→ Supports Pupil Book Investigation, page 27

Unit 5 Travel

Lesson 2: Finding your way

1 Complete the sentences using words from the boxes.

| scale | grid | landmarks | route |

a) The _____ of a map shows how the distance on the map matches the actual distance on the ground.

b) The _____ is the path or way you take to get from one place to another.

c) A _____ on a street map makes it easier to find places.

d) Shops, rivers and parks are examples of _____ shown on some maps.

2 Which type of map would you need for these activities? What information would the map need to show?

a) Walking

Type of map: _____

Information it needs to show: _____

b) Travelling across the country by train

Type of map: _____

Information it needs to show: _____

c) Delivering a parcel in a city

Type of map: _____

Information it needs to show: _____

d) Planning a new town

Type of map: _____

Information it needs to show: _____

Unit 5 Travel

3 Look at the street map and find these places. Write the grid references.

a) Train station _____

b) Shopping centre _____

c) Hospital _____

d) Park _____

e) Market _____

f) School _____

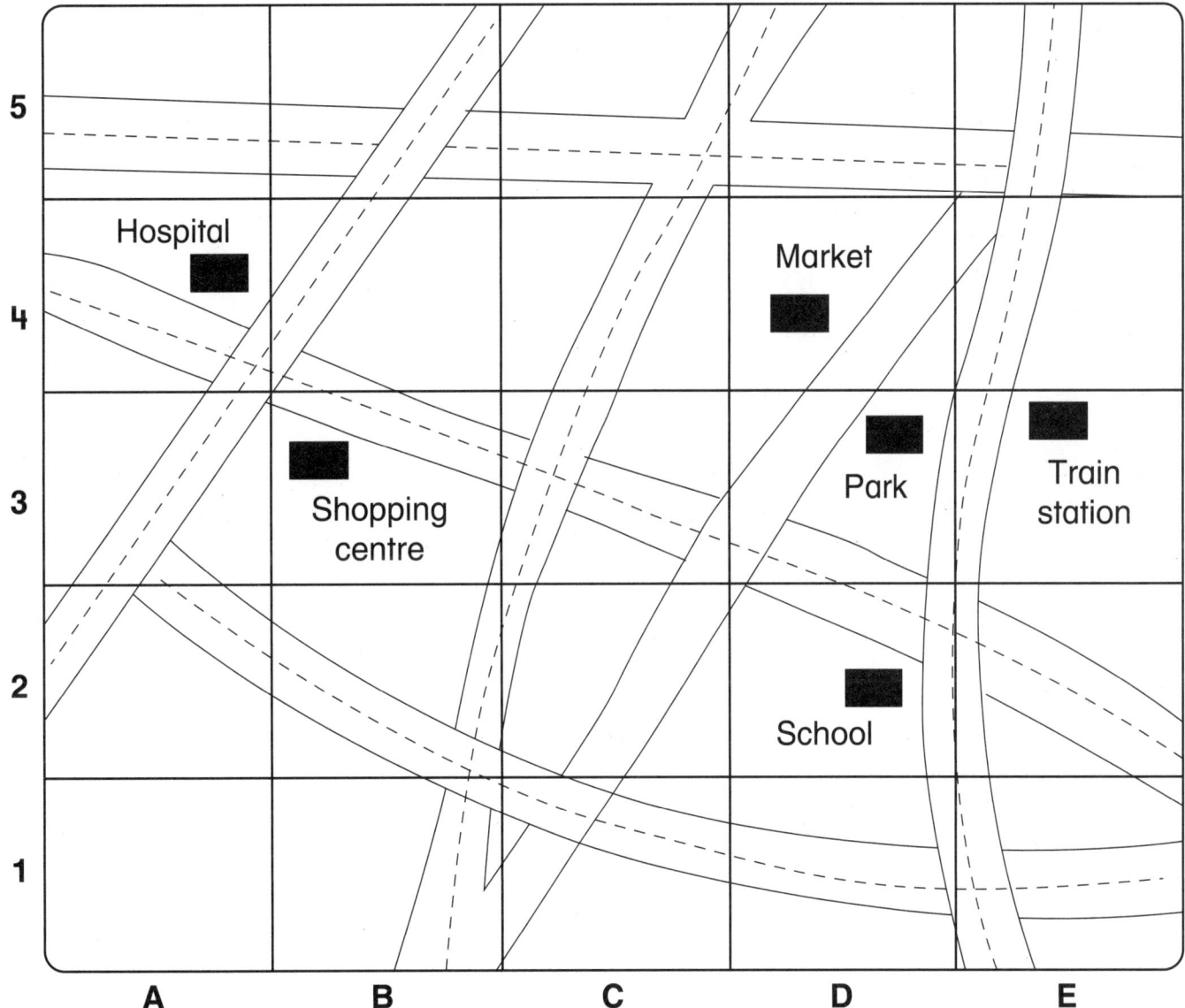

Unit 5 Travel

Lesson 3: Routes and journeys

1 Complete the map below to show your routes through the town.

a) You are at the station. You walk from the station and past the shops. Then you take a bus to school. Draw your route.

b) After school you walk to Pedro's house. Draw your route.

c) Then you walk to Malia's house. You do not take the roads or paths. Draw your route.

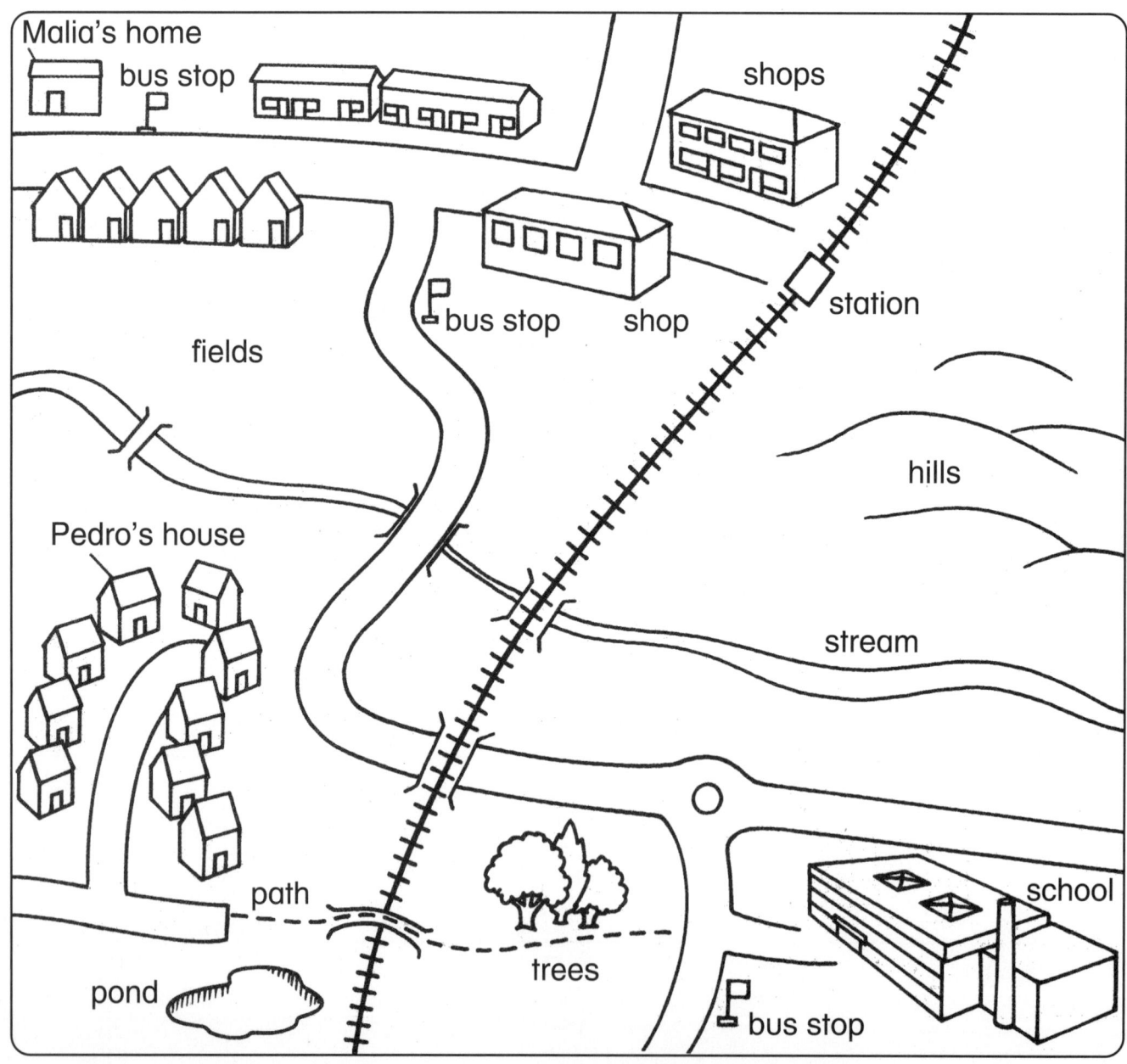

Hint: Use a different colour for each of the three routes.

Unit 5 Travel

❷ You are going to draw a map which shows the route you take to school.

Before you draw the map, answer these questions.

Hint: Do you go by bus? Do you walk? Or do you go by another form of transport?

a) How do you get to school?

_____

b) What landmarks do you pass on the way to school? Make a list.

_____   _____

_____   _____

❸ Draw your map. Label the landmarks. Show your route along the map.

→ Supports Pupil Book Mapwork, page 31

Unit 6 Caring for nature

Lesson 1: Wildlife around us

1 Make a survey of small animals that live near your home.

    a) Draw pictures of five small living creatures that you think you will find. Write the name under each picture. (Example: spider)

    b) Where does each animal live? Draw pictures or write the names of the habitats. Some animals may live in the same habitats. (Example: under some bushes)

    c) Visit the places. Did you find the animals? How many did you find? (Example: 0, 2, etc.)

Animals	Habitat (where they live)	How many did you find?
1.		
2.		
3.		
4.		
5.		

Unit 6 Caring for nature

❷ Draw a block graph to show what you found in your survey.
- Write the name of each habitat at the bottom of the columns.
- Colour in the number of blocks to show how many animals you found in each habitat. Use different colours for each habitat.

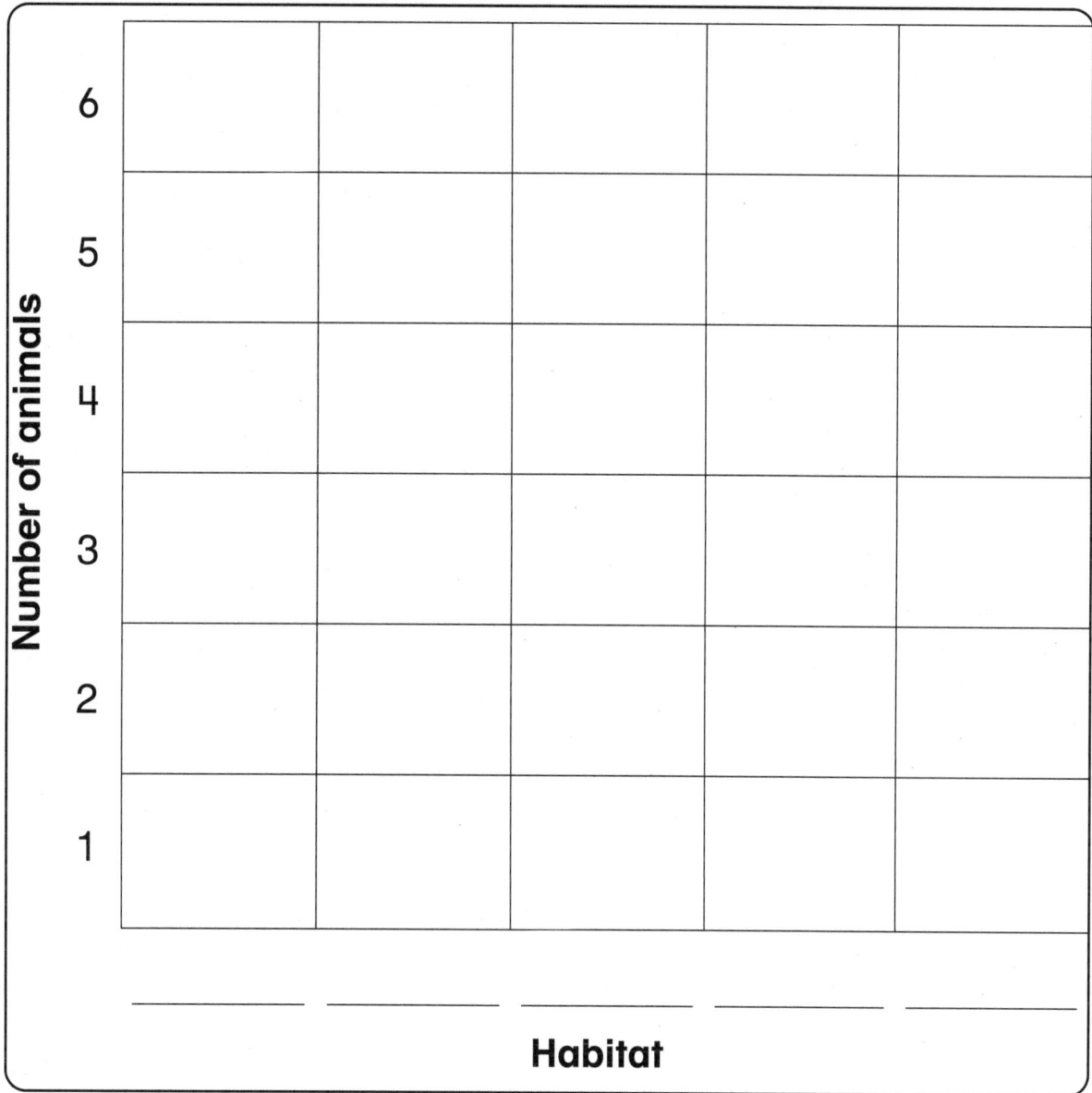

❸ Write about your investigation.

a) In which habitat did you find the most animals?

_____

b) Make a list of the animals you found in this habitat.

_____

c) Why do you think the animals live in this habitat?

_____

Unit 6 **Caring for nature**

Lesson 2: Protecting wildlife

❶ Draw lines to match the words to their meanings.

conservation		The world around us.
environment		Anything that makes the environment dirtier or damaging to people, plants or animals.
habitat		A place where animals and plants are protected.
pollution		The place where plants and animals live.
a reserve		Looking after plants and animals, and saving habitats.

❷ a) Use the internet or a library to find out more about one of the conservation projects from pages 34 and 35 of your Pupil Book. Which animals and plants are protected in the project? Write the name of one plant and one animal that interests you.

Plant: _____   Animal: _____

b) Draw a picture of the plant and the animal. Write a sentence about each picture.

→ Supports Pupil Book Climate change, page 34

34

Unit 6 Caring for nature

3 What wild plants and animals need to be protected in the country where you live?

Hint: Ask an adult or use the internet.

_____

4 Look at these posters. What are they encouraging people to do?

Poster A: _____

Poster B: _____

5 What can you do to encourage people to care for wildlife? Draw your own poster to show your idea. Include a heading.

→ Supports Pupil Book Investigation, page 35

Unit 6 Caring for nature

Lesson 3: Working together

❶ Write the plants and animals that you might see on this trail around a school.

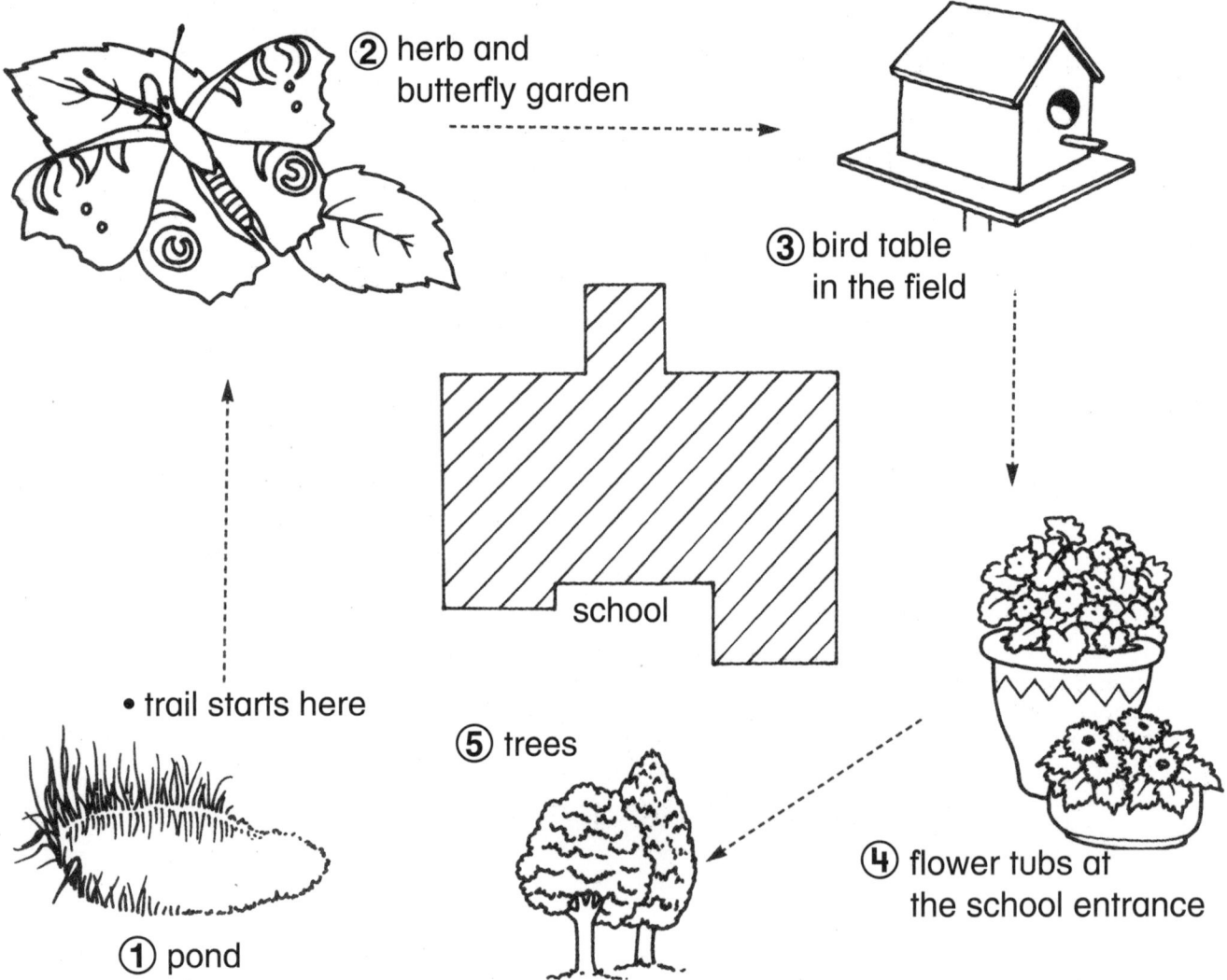

Stop	What animals might you see at this place?
1	
2	
3	
4	
5	

Unit 6 **Caring for nature**

❷ Draw a plan of a garden for your school.

Think about these questions:

- How could you work together with your class to make and look after the garden?
- Which flowers would attract birds and insects?
- Which plants would provide shelter for animals?
- Where would the plants get water?
- How would you use the garden?

❸ Draw a trail through the garden on your plan.

❹ What **four** things in the garden would you like people to see?

1. _____
2. _____
3. _____
4. _____

➜ Supports Pupil Book Investigation, page 37

Unit 7 Scotland

Lesson 1: Introducing Scotland

❶ Label these islands on the map.

> Orkney Islands   Outer Hebrides   Shetland Islands

❷ Add these mountains and rivers to the map.

> Grampian Mountains   River Forth   River Clyde

Hint: Look at Pupil Book page 38 if you need help.

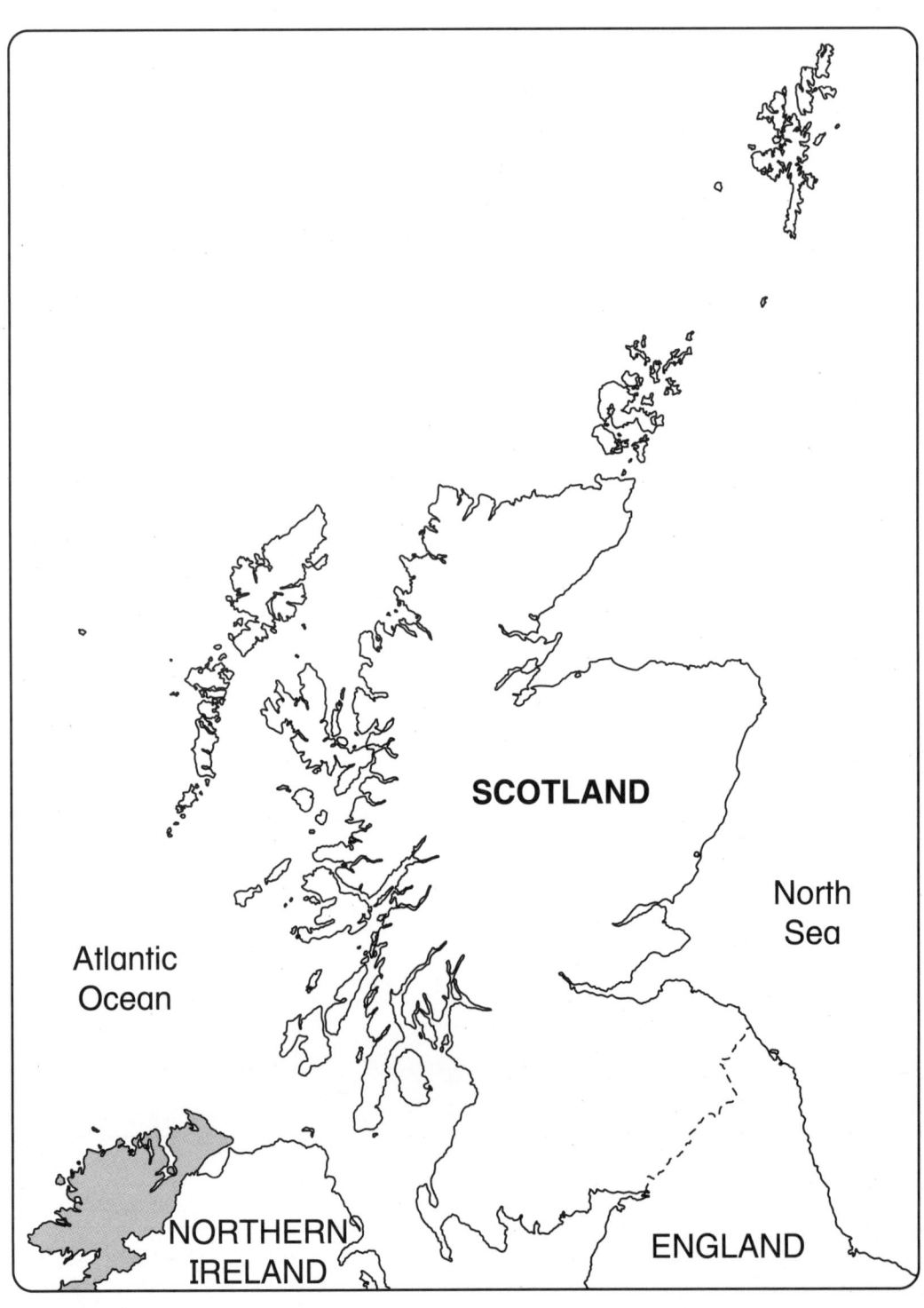

Unit 7 Scotland

❸ Answer the questions.

a) Is Scotland in the northern or eastern part of the United Kingdom?
_____

b) Which coasts of Scotland have lots of islands: north, south, east or west?
_____

c) Where are the lowlands: top, middle or bottom?
_____

d) Some wind farms are in the sea. Why is the sea a good place for wind farms?
_____

❹ Complete the notes on **Tourism in Scotland**. Add more information when you have completed your own investigation.

Tourism in Scotland	
How many tourists visit each year?	number is growing
Which places in Scotland do tourists like to visit?	Edinburgh
What do tourists enjoy about Scotland?	hiking in the mountains
Why is tourism important for Scotland?	

→ Supports Pupil Book Investigation, page 39

Unit 7 Scotland

Lesson 2: Edinburgh: The capital city of Scotland

1 Look at the photographs of two Edinburgh landmarks and complete the information.

Name	Where is it in Scotland?	Why is it important?
Edinburgh Castle	_____	_____
Firth of Forth bridges	_____	_____

2 Name three places in Edinburgh that you would like to visit. Write a sentence about why you would like to visit them.

a) Place: _____

I would like to visit because _____.

b) Place: _____

I would like to visit because _____.

c) Place: _____

I would like to visit because _____.

→ Supports Pupil Book Investigation, page 41

Unit 7 Scotland

3 Name two types of work that people in the city of Edinburgh can do.

_____

_____

4 Give three ways tourists can get to Edinburgh.

_____

_____

_____

5 Choose the best word to complete each sentence. Colour the answer.

a) Arthur's Seat was once a …

(waterfall) (bridge) (volcano) (river)

b) … is a railway station in Edinburgh.

(Haymarket) (Andrews) (Royal Mile) (Holyrood)

c) One of the main streets in Edinburgh is …

(Lismore Street) (Adderley Street)

(Charlotte Street) (Princes Street)

6 Read the sentences about Edinburgh. Are they true or false? Colour the answer.

a) Edinburgh is a town in England.   (True) (False)

b) Edinburgh is the capital city of Scotland.   (True) (False)

c) Edinburgh is a very old city.   (True) (False)

Unit 7 Scotland

Lesson 3: Mull: A Scottish island

1 Draw lines to match the words with the pictures.

cliff

lighthouse

croft

moor

ferry

2 Read the sentences about the Isle of Mull. Are they true or false? Colour the answer.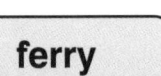

a) There are steep cliffs along the coastline.   True   False

b) There are moors only on the northern coast of the island.   True   False

c) A croft is a mountain.   True   False

3 What could you do if you visited the Isle of Mull?

_____

_____

4 What items of clothing would you pack to visit the island? Explain why.

_____

_____

Unit 7 **Scotland**

❺ Look at the map of Mull in western Scotland. Plan a visit for yourself or a tourist.

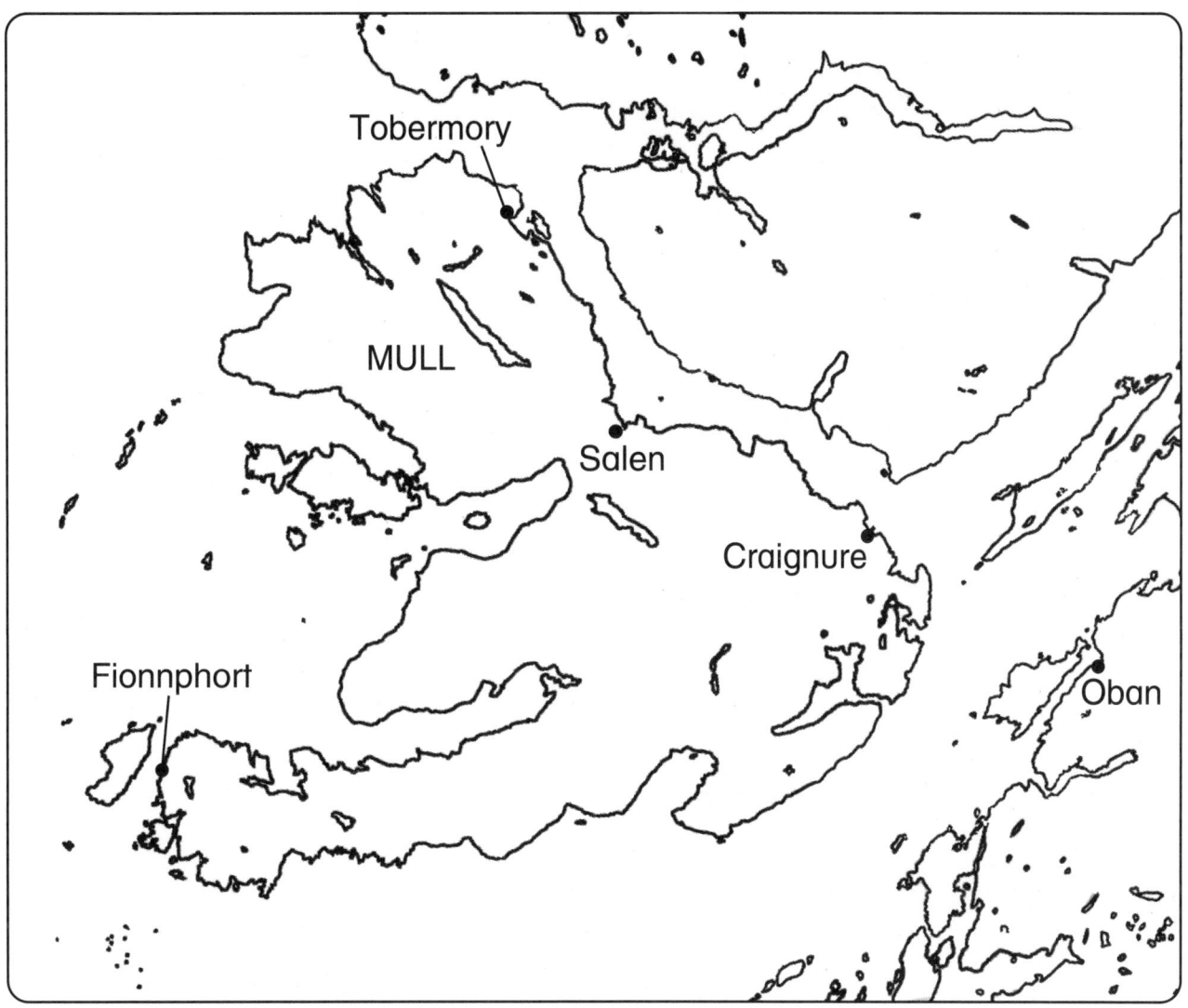

a) Which places will you visit?

_____

b) Where can you start?

_____

c) How would you get from one place to the next?

_____

d) What activities will you do?

_____

❻ Plot your route on the map.

→ Supports Pupil Book Investigation, page 43

Unit 8 France

Lesson 1: Introducing France

1 Complete the key with a symbol for mountains and the colour blue for seas and oceans.

2 a) Add mountains in the correct places to the map of France. Use the symbol from your key.

b) Colour the seas and oceans using the colour from your key.

3 Add these labels to the map:

Atlantic Ocean   English Channel   Alps

Mediterranean Sea   Paris   Pyrenees

Key

mountains	
seas and oceans	

Hint: Look at the map on Pupil Book page 44.

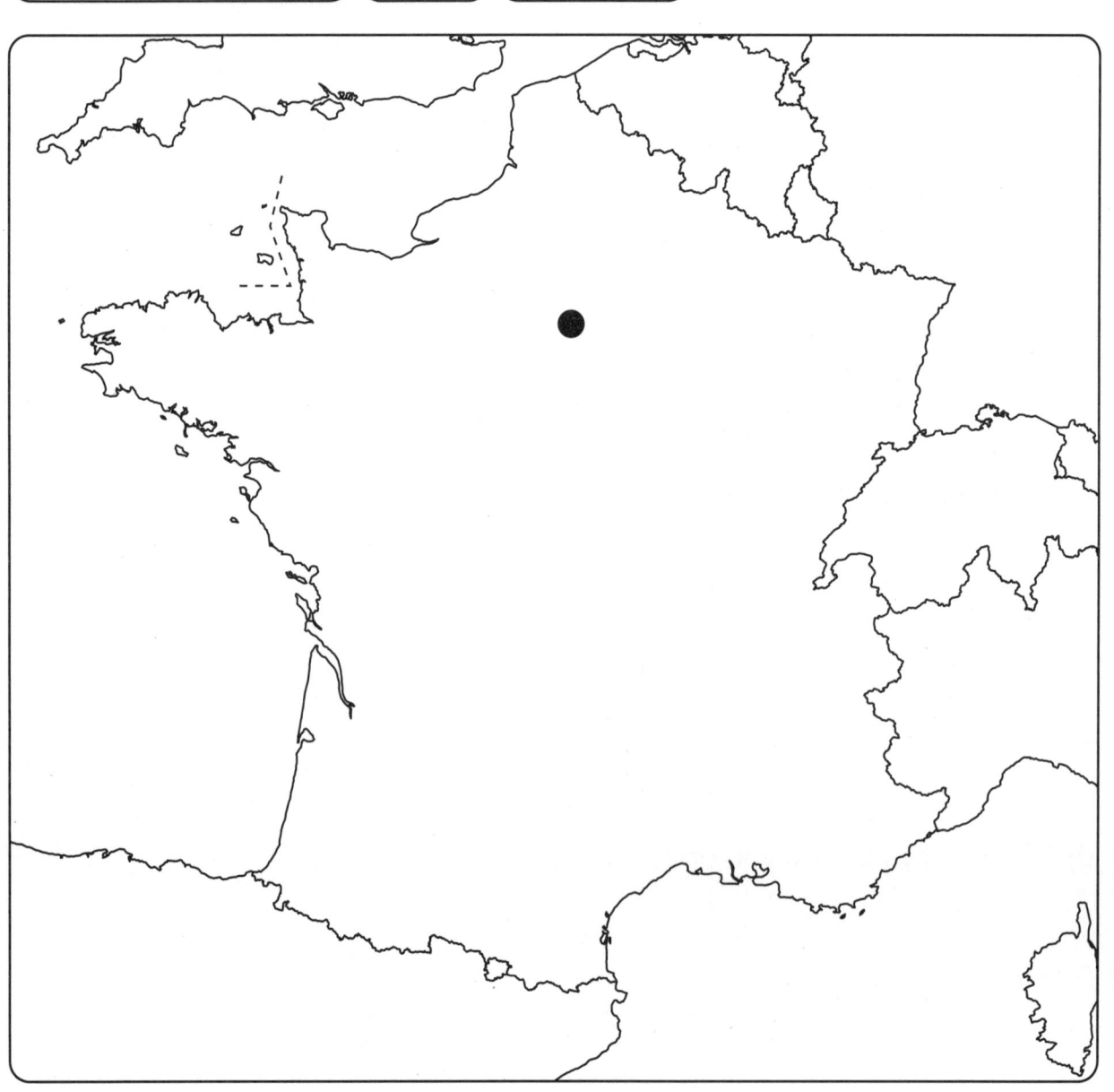

Unit 8 France

4) What do these photographs tell us about France? Write a sentence about each photograph.

a) _____

b) _____

5) Complete the paragraph about France. Use the words from the boxes.

| industries | south | Alps | Loire | Paris |

France is a country in Europe. The capital city is _____. It has high mountain ranges such as the _____ and the Pyrenees. The longest rivers are the Seine, the _____, the Garonne and the Rhône. France has many farms as well as big _____. The north of France is often quite wet, while the _____ is hot and dry.

45

Unit 8 France

Lesson 2: Growing food

1 Find or draw pictures of two important crops in France. Write a sentence about each picture.

a) _____

b) _____

2 Why do farmers raise cows and goats in France?

_____

3 What makes the village of Parnac a good place for growing food? Tick ✓ two sentences.

a) The soil is fertile because it is in a river valley. ☐

b) There are high mountains with snow. ☐

c) The climate is good with plenty of sunshine. ☐

4 Parnac is in the south-west of France. Use an atlas or the internet to find out:

a) How far away it is from Paris.

_____

b) The names of two towns near to Parnac.

_____ _____

Unit 8 France

5 Compare the area where you live to the area of Parnac in France. Complete the table.

	Your area	Parnac
Settlement Is it a village, a city or a town?		
Climate Is it hot, cold, wet or dry?		
Landscape Are there mountains, rivers or valleys?		
Transport How do you get to and from the area?		
Work How do people earn a living?		

6 Write two sentences about crops that are grown in the country where you live.

_____

_____

_____

_____

Unit 8   France

Lesson 3: Making cars

Reread the information on pages 48 and 49 of your Pupil Book.

1 Look at the map, then answer the questions.

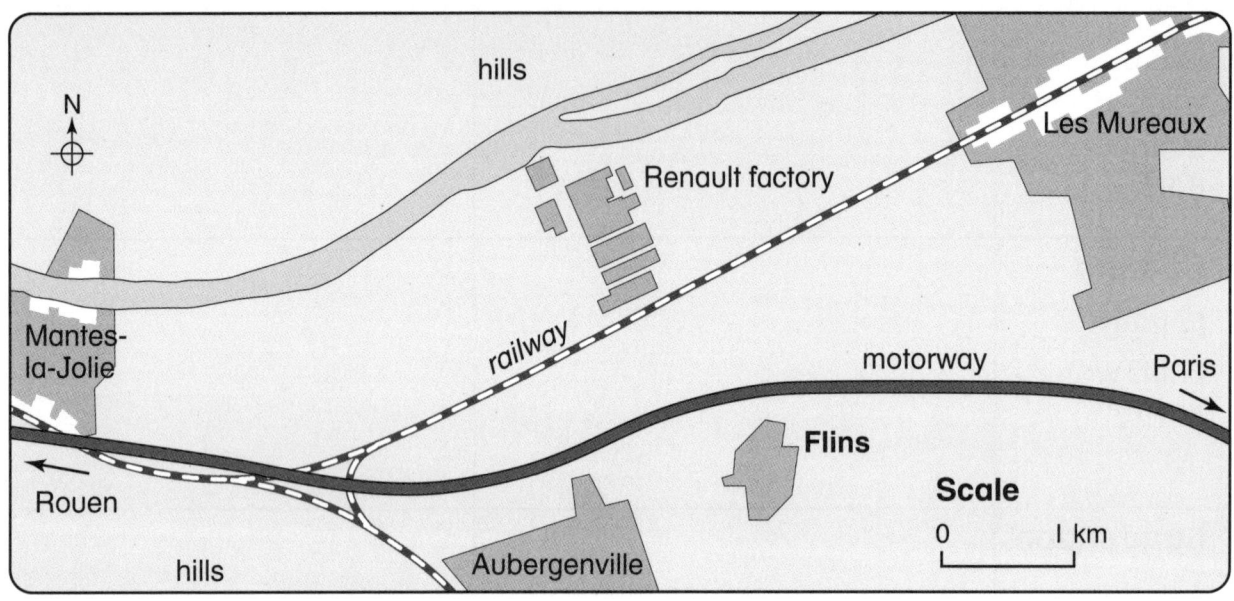

a) What does the factory in Flins make?

_____

b) How far is Flins from Paris?

_____

c) Which big river is near the town?

_____

d) Why is this a good place for a factory?

_____

_____

e) What might happen to people in Flins if the factory closed?

_____

_____

_____

→ Supports Pupil Book Discussion, page 48

Unit 8 | France

❷ Complete the diagram.

The production cycle at a sustainable car factory

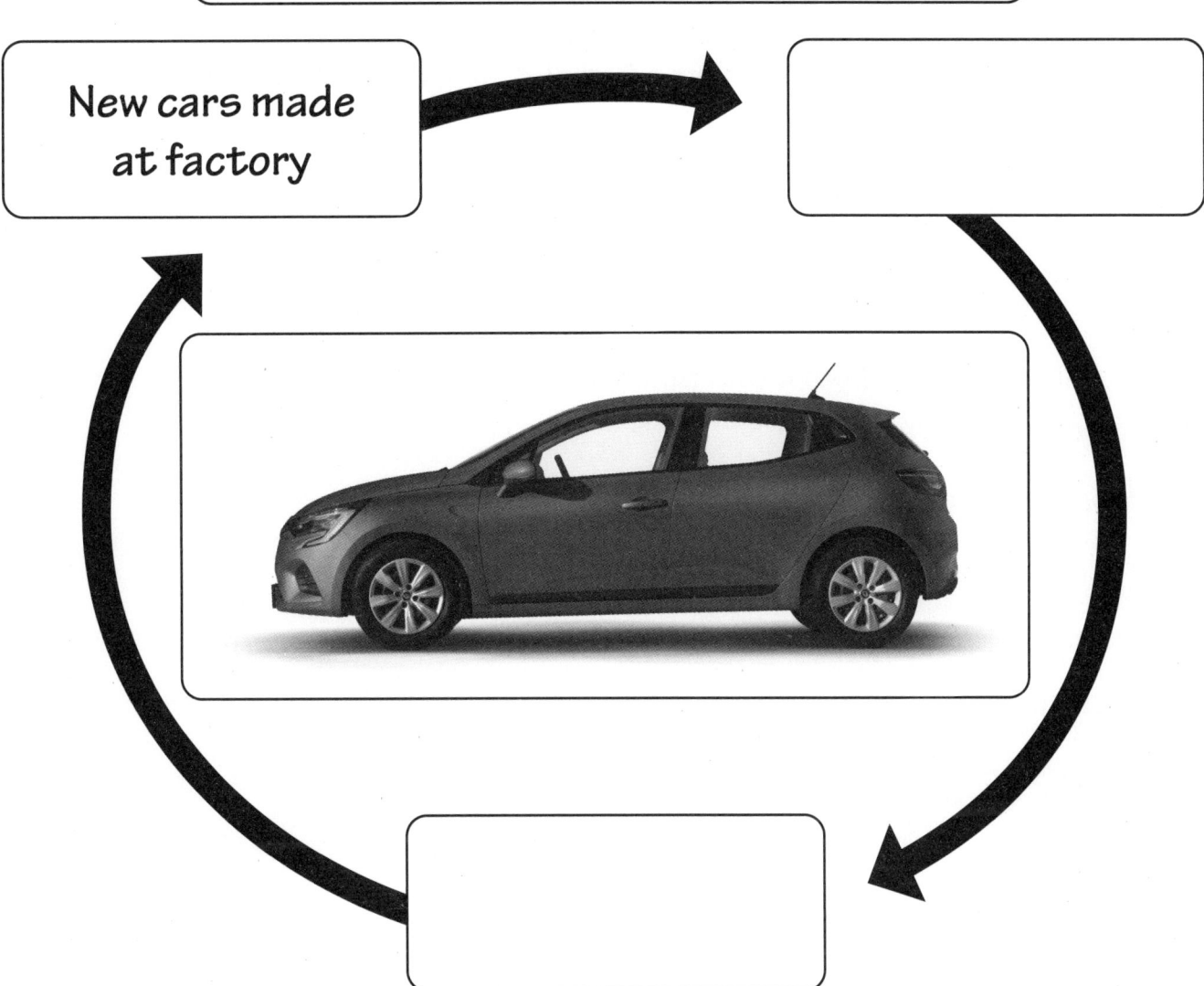

New cars made at factory

❸ It is necessary to change the way we use and make cars because the old ways harm the environment. How does the new factory at Flins do less harm to the environment? List three ways.

_____

_____

_____

→ Supports Pupil Book Climate change, page 49

Unit 9　South America

Lesson 1: Introducing South America

1 Colour the names of nine places or features that are in South America.

- Andes
- Panama Canal
- River Amazon
- River Nile
- Lake Titicaca
- Brazil
- Peru
- Spain
- Bolivia
- Argentina
- River Orinoco
- Alps

2 Complete the quiz about South America.

True or false? Write T or F.

a) Bolivia is below (south of) the equator. _____

b) Lima is in Brazil. _____

c) The River Amazon flows into the Atlantic Ocean. _____

d) Brazil is the biggest country. _____

e) There are large areas of rainforest around the River Amazon. _____

f) Argentina is above (north of) the equator. _____

g) Buenos Aires is in Argentina. _____

h) More people live in the countryside than in cities. _____

i) Ships cannot sail on Lake Titicaca. _____

j) There are desert areas in South America. _____

Hint: Look at the map and Data bank on Pupil Book page 51.

Unit 9 South America

3 Write two facts about each of these places and features in South America. Write notes or short sentences about each.

a) The River Amazon

_____

_____

_____

b) The Andes

_____

_____

_____

c) Brazil

_____

_____

_____

d) Lake Titicaca

_____

_____

_____

4 Use an atlas or the internet to find the names of five countries in South America that have parts that are north of the equator.

_____

_____

_____

_____

_____

Unit 9 — South America

Lesson 2: Spotlight on Chile

1 Draw lines to match the words to their definitions.

desert	an opening which lava, rocks and gas can erupt from
volcano	a long, narrow valley flooded with water
geyser	an area where the water is hotter than the air around it
fjord	a dry area where there is very little rain
glacier	this shoots steam and hot water up into the air
hot springs	a large, thick river of ice that stays frozen

2 Write the name of the country where you live at the top of the third column. Then compare Chile and your country. Tick ✓ the columns if the answer is yes.

	Chile	_____
Are there copper mines?		
Are there salmon farms?		
Are there vineyards?		
Are there any fjords?		
Are there active volcanoes?		
Are there deserts?		

→ Supports Pupil Book Investigation, page 53

Unit 9 South America

3 Follow the instructions to complete the map.

Hint: Look at the maps on Pupil Book page 52.

a) Draw the outline of Chile on the map.

b) Copy these words into the key. Add a different colour for each one.

Andes Mountains   forest   farmland   desert

c) Show where the places from part b) are on the map. Use drawings and the colours in the key.

d) Label the ocean to the west of Chile.

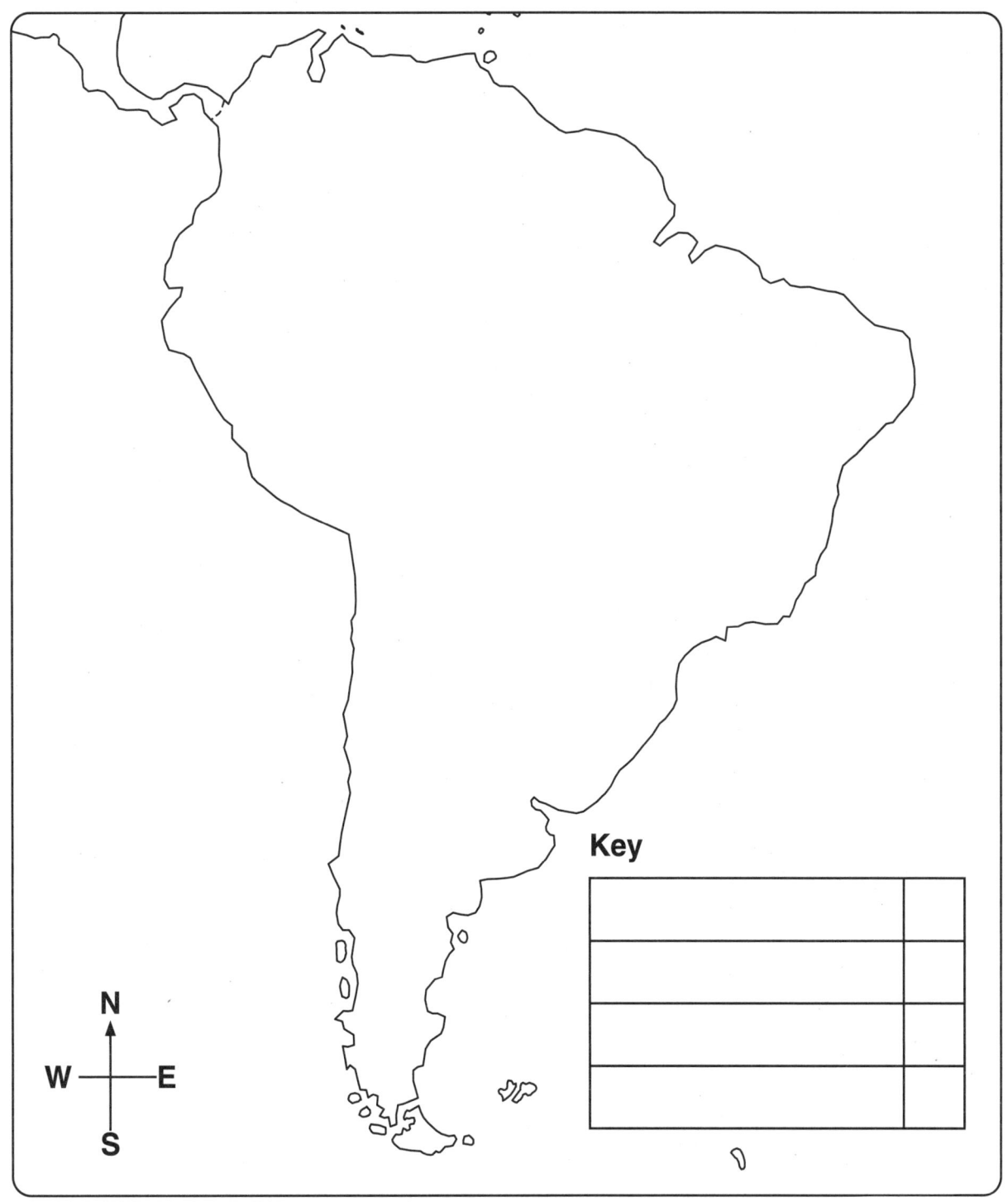

Key

53

Unit 9 — South America

Lesson 3: The Galapagos Islands

1 Add the information to the map of the Galapagos Islands.

Hint: Look at the map on Pupil Book page 54.

a) Add labels for the names of these islands:

- Santiago Island
- Santa Cruz Island
- San Cristóbal Island
- Isabela Island

b) Draw the equator. Use a ruler.

c) Add a label with the name of the ocean.

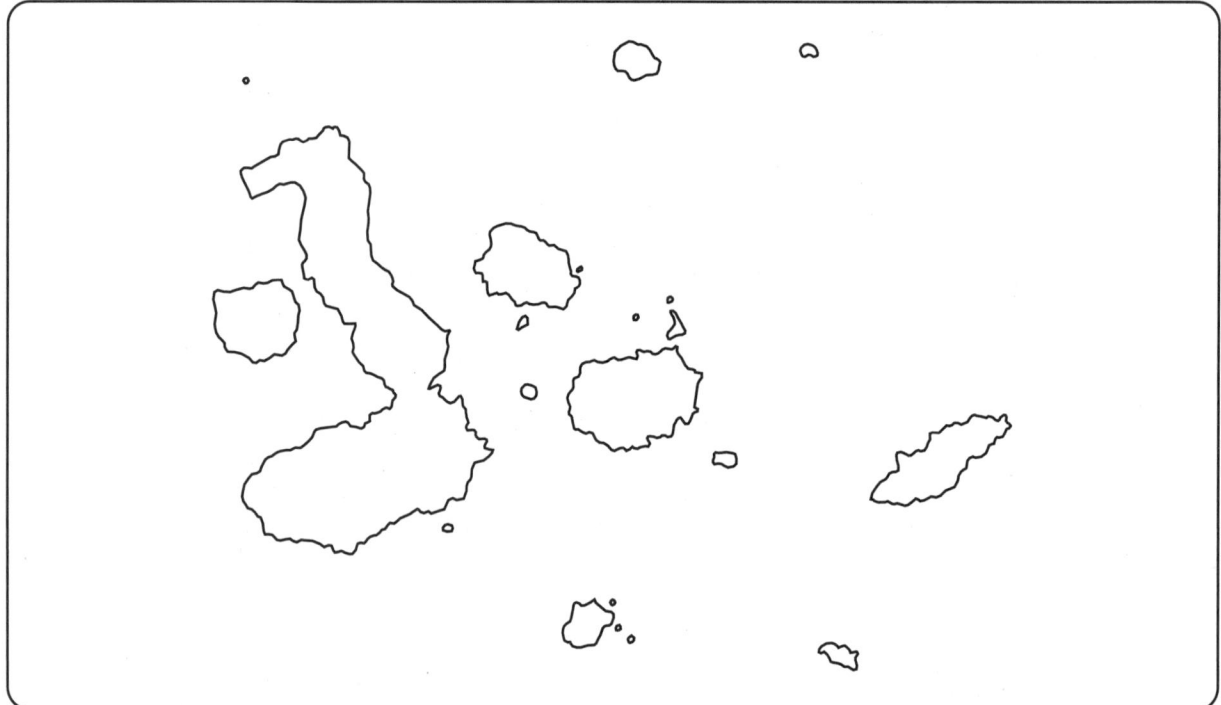

2 Complete the paragraph about the Galapagos Islands using the words from the boxes.

- balance
- equator
- west
- summit
- Heritage

The Galapagos Islands are found to the _____ of the country of Ecuador in South America. The islands are the _____ of an underwater volcano. There are over one hundred islands in the Galapagos and they are a World _____ Site. The islands are on both sides of the _____. Tourism is controlled because too many visitors would upset the _____ of life on the islands.

Unit 9 South America

3 Write the names of three animals that live in the Galapagos.

_____   _____   _____

4 The photographs below show an animal and a plant that are found in the Galapagos.

a) Do some research and find interesting information about them.

b) Write two sentences about each picture.

A Galapagos penguin on Isabela Island

Prickly Pear (Opuntia) cacti on Santa Cruz Island

→ Supports Pupil Book Investigation, page 55

Unit 10   Asia

Lesson 1: Introducing Asia

1 Read the clues and complete the crossword puzzle.

Across

2   A big country in Asia.   I _ _ _ _

6   A long range of mountains with high peaks.   H _ _ _ _ _ _ _ _

8   A big city in China.   S _ _ _ _ _ _

Down

1   A very cold place where there are pine trees and swamps.   S _ _ _ _ _ _

3   A big country in Asia.   C _ _ _ _

4   A large desert in Asia.   G _ _ _

5   A big country in northern Asia.   R _ _ _ _ _ _

7   The rains that come in July.   M _ _ _ _ _ _ _

Unit 10   Asia

❷ Find or draw pictures of landscapes in Asia to match the words.

mountain	
desert	
grassland	
forest	

→ Supports Pupil Book Investigation, page 57

❸ Choose two of the landscapes from Activity 2. Write a caption to describe each picture.

a) _____

b) _____

Unit 10 Asia

Lesson 2: India: A country in Asia

1 What have you learnt about India? Read the clues, then find the answers in the wordsearch puzzle.

Hint: Look at the map and information on Pupil Book page 58.

a) A long range of high mountains in the north. _ _ _ _ _ _ _ _ _

b) The biggest river. River _ _ _ _ _ _

c) The capital city. New _ _ _ _ _

d) The name of a desert in the west. _ _ _ _ Desert

e) The national sport. _ _ _ _ _ _ _

f) A city on the Bay of Bengal. K _ _ _ _ _ _

g) A big city on the west coast. M _ _ _ _ _

h) The sea along the west coast. _ _ _ _ _ _ _ Sea

j	v	q	p	x	d	z	j	e	q
c	r	i	c	k	e	t	q	x	g
q	m	v	k	o	l	k	a	t	a
x	u	z	b	v	h	j	r	p	n
p	m	j	x	z	i	v	a	b	g
v	b	t	h	a	r	q	b	k	e
k	a	p	b	q	k	x	i	p	s
h	i	m	a	l	a	y	a	s	j
z	j	z	q	j	v	t	n	q	v
u	k	b	n	a	q	o	v	x	p

58

Unit 10 Asia

❷ Use an atlas to find countries which surround India. Use the names of the countries in the boxes to label the map.

China   Pakistan   Nepal   Bangladesh
Bhutan   Myanmar (Burma)   Afghanistan   Sri Lanka

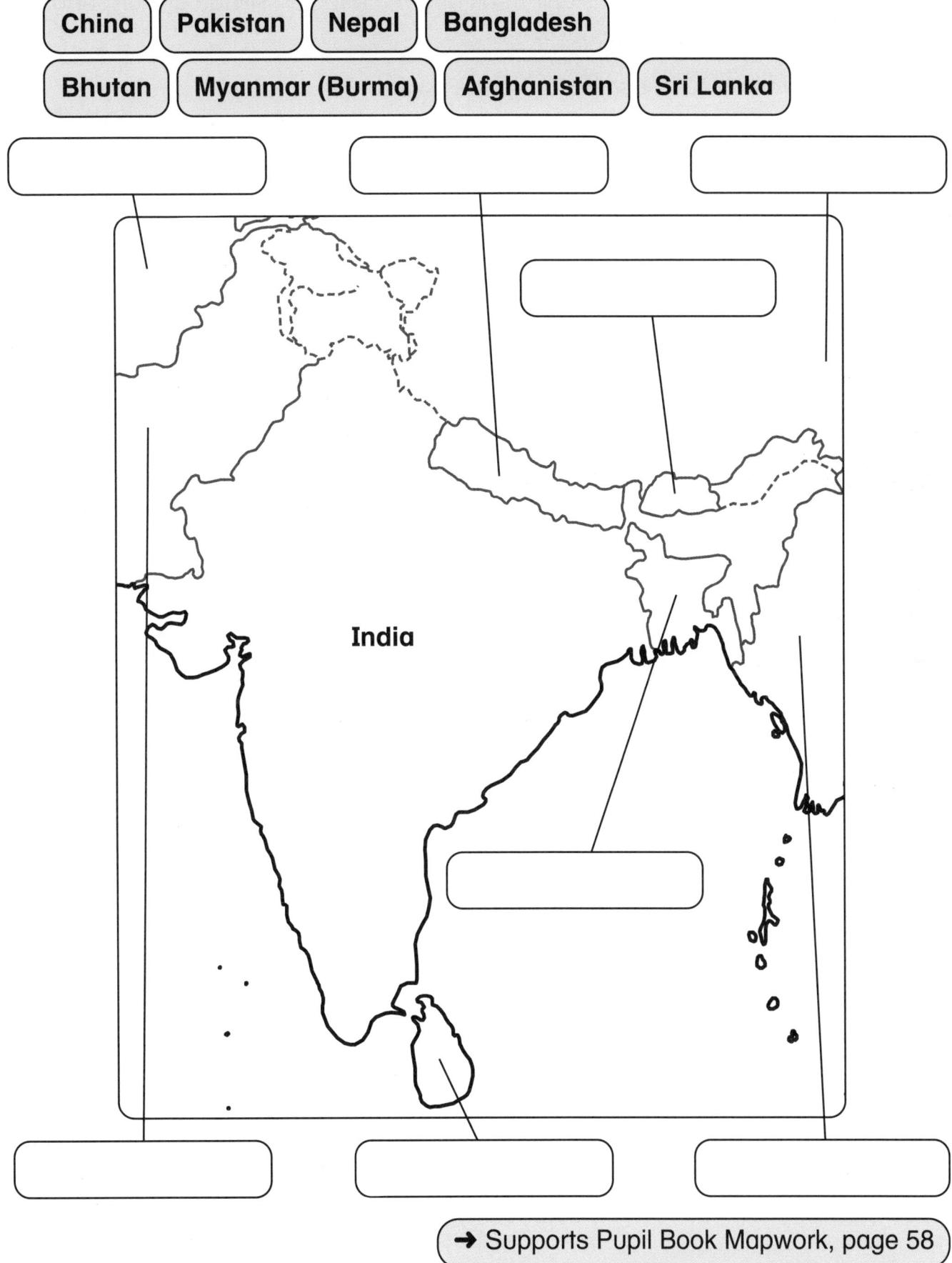

→ Supports Pupil Book Mapwork, page 58

Unit 10 Asia

Lesson 3: Pallipadu: A village in India

Reread pages 59 to 61 of your Pupil Book about the Indian village of Pallipadu.

1 Complete the map of Pallipadu.

a) Draw symbols for these places in the boxes.

shop	**well**	**post office**	**banyan tree**

b) Draw the places from part **a)** on the map.

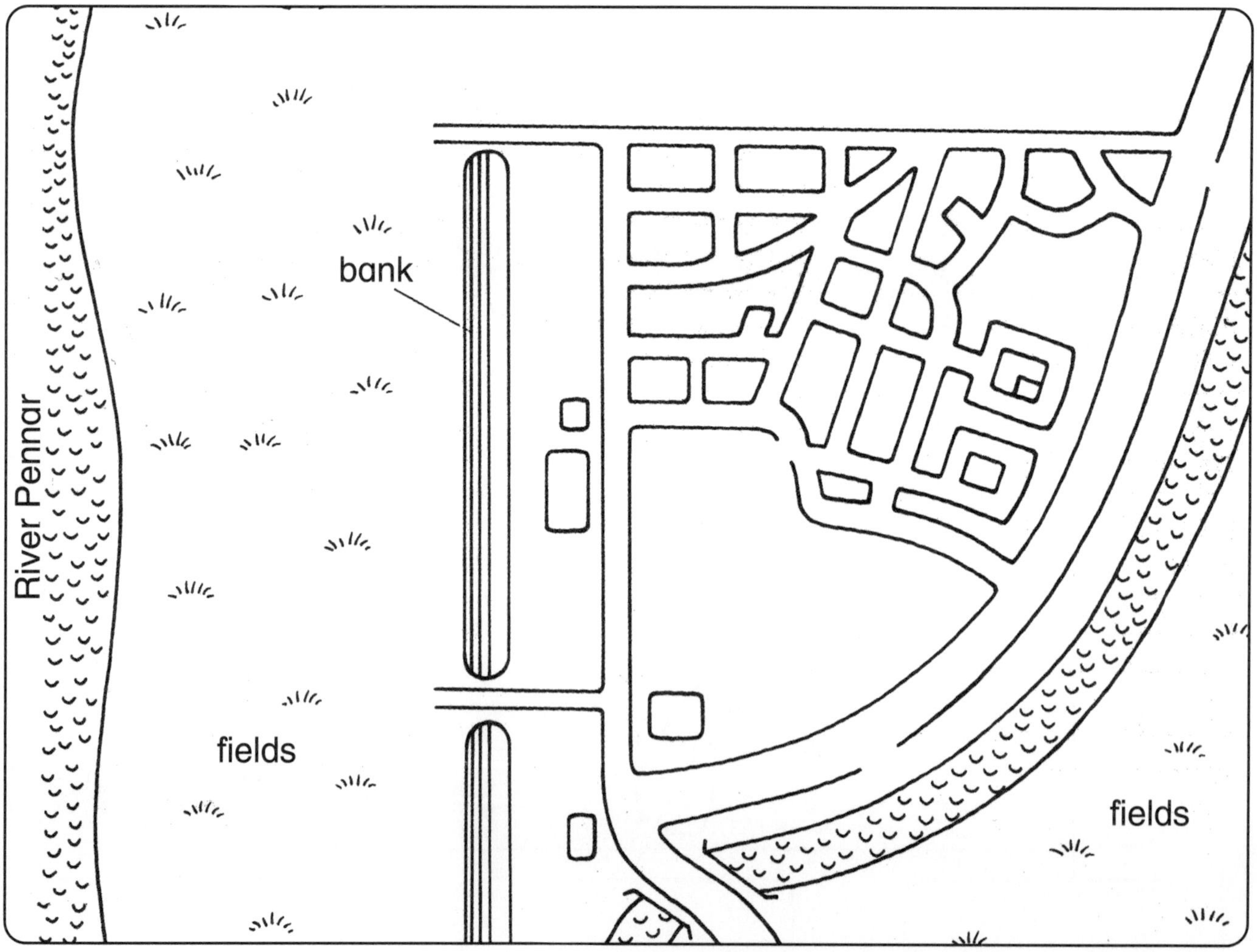

→ Supports Pupil Book Mapwork, page 60

Unit 10 Asia

2 What two things make sure there is a safe supply of water in Pallipadu?

_____

_____

3 Imagine you are visiting Pallipadu. Write an email to a friend. Describe what you saw on your visit.

Hint: You can describe the places, houses, farming activities and transport used.

From: _____

To: _____

Subject: _____

_____
_____
_____
_____
_____
_____
_____
_____
_____
_____

→ Supports Pupil Book Investigation, page 61

Notes

William Collins' dream of knowledge for all began with the publication of his first book in 1819.

A self-educated mill worker, he not only enriched millions of lives, but also founded a flourishing publishing house. Today, staying true to this spirit, Collins books are packed with inspiration, innovation and practical expertise.
They place you at the centre of a world of possibility and give you exactly what you need to explore it.

Published by Collins
An imprint of HarperCollins*Publishers*
The News Building, 1 London Bridge Street, London, SE1 9GF, UK

HarperCollins*Publishers*
Macken House, 39/40 Mayor Street Upper, Dublin 1, D01 C9W8, Ireland

Browse the complete Collins catalogue at
collins.co.uk

© HarperCollins*Publishers* Limited 2025
Maps © Collins Bartholomew 2025

10 9 8 7 6 5 4 3 2 1

ISBN 978-0-00-872836-6

All rights reserved. No part of this publication may be reproduced, stored in a retrieval system, or transmitted in any form by any means, electronic, mechanical, photocopying, recording or otherwise, without the prior written permission of the Publisher or a licence permitting restricted copying in the United Kingdom issued by the Copyright Licensing Agency Ltd, 5th Floor, Shackleton House, 4 Battle Bridge Lane, London SE1 2HX.

Without limiting the author's and publisher's exclusive rights, any unauthorised use of this publication to train generative artificial intelligence (AI) technologies is expressly prohibited. HarperCollins also exercise their rights under Article 4(3) of the Digital Single Market Directive 2019/790 and expressly reserve this publication from the text and data mining exception.

British Library Cataloguing-in-Publication Data

A catalogue record for this publication is available from the British Library.

Author: Daphne Paizee
Publisher: Laura White
Product managers: Natasha Paul and Shelley Teasdale
Development editor: Judith Walters
Copyeditor: Charlotte Christensen
Proofreader: Charlotte Christensen
Cover designer and illustrator: Steve Evans
Internal illustrator: Jouve India Private Ltd
Typesetter: David Jimenez
Production controller: Katie Jean-Baptiste
Printed and bound in the UK by Martins the Printers

MIX
Paper | Supporting responsible forestry
FSC™ C007454

This book is produced from independently certified FSC™ paper to ensure responsible forest management.

For more information visit: www.harpercollins.co.uk/green collins.co.uk/sustainability

Acknowledgements

The publishers gratefully acknow5ledge the permission granted to reproduce the copyright material in this book. Every effort has been made to trace copyright holders and to obtain their permission for the use of copyright material. The publishers will gladly receive any information enabling them to rectify any error or omission at the first opportunity.

All photos: Shutterstock.